Adam Chodzko

Plans and Spells

Film and Video Umbrella

Adam Chodzko: Plans and Spells

Steven Bode

In Umberto Eco's novel 'Foucault's Pendulum', a trio of editors at one of Milan's more esoteric publishing houses are handed an anonymous manuscript which purports to have discovered an intricate and mysterious plan, originally formulated by the medieval knights of the Templars, and said to grant its practitioners prodigious supernatural powers. Bored with their daily diet of crackpot theories by second-rate occultists, the editors hit upon an amusing idea: namely, to pool their not inconsiderable knowledge of arcane literature, feed it into a computer, programme the machine to edit it at random, and see what comes out. To their delight, the computer regurgitates the material in striking and arresting ways, which, with little more than minor explication from themselves, can be made to disclose a secret history of the last seven hundred years. After a while, though, their miraculous brainchild (which our modern-day Magi dub the 'Plan') starts to draw them under its spell – so much so that the trio begin to wonder whether this play of chance and connection is really just an accident or actually part of some inexorably unfolding, and extraordinarily revelatory, Grand Design.

At first glance, it seems as if Adam Chodzko might be attempting something similar in his video installation, *Plan for a Spell*. Images and sounds culled from locations across Britain (highlighting some of the more haunting and numinous places in the landscape but also drawing our attention to more obviously familiar everyday events) are encoded onto a DVD in such a way that all its sequences combine randomly and infinitely. Shots of the surviving stumps of ancient pagan figures might therefore appear next to wind turbines turning on a hilltop, or, less portentously perhaps, a burning funeral pyre of diseased cattle might collide with images of stock-car racing. The resonant nature of the material (including traditional rituals such as fire ceremonies, with their roots in a mythical pantheistic past) ensures that, while these juxtapositions are always entirely random, an underlying pattern often seems as if it's about to emerge. This trail of meaning, which resembles the psychogeographical ramblings of a non-metropolitan flâneur, may, at times, appear elusive and opaque; but, for those who are ready to see them, coincidences lurk beneath the surface, connecting and proliferating like a network of ley-lines.

As the piece unravels (flitting haphazardly through its index of images, some of which are repeated at irregular intervals, although, this time, with different soundtracks), sequences are overlaid with a series of equally halting and meandering subtitles. More conversational than conspiratorial, these sporadic interjections from an endearingly diffident master of

ceremonies ('So, not this bit… not yet… we'll reach it soon though, I think… Maybe you're noticing some changes by now. I guess it depends what comes next…') add to the sense that this hubbub of material will, eventually, cohere, and that something remarkable, maybe even magical, will occur. Although there is a chance that this all may be a figment of the narrator's overactive imagination, it is just as likely that these complex and evolving permutations are actually part of an elaborate code; one that is proceeding according to numerological principles or configured around the secret logic of a cabbala.

Codes have always been a source of fascination for Chodzko – the knack of being both intriguingly cryptic and immediately accessible is a defining feature of his work (a trick, incidentally, that comparatively few people have managed to pull off; the literary semiotician turned popular novelist, Eco, being one of the names that stands out). Sometimes, as in *Better Scenery* or *The God Look-Alike Contest*, Chodzko's pieces play with the arbitrary nature of systems of meaning, as if to highlight their basic absurdity. In others, such as *Nightvision* or *Secretors*, he invents, or introduces, a coded idiom of his own: gnomic, ludic, hermetic but always capable of producing startling, or unsettling, transformative effects, especially when let loose in the public domain. Intensely methodical but ultimately wholly unclassifiable, no artist's work is more deserving of the epithet 'more than the sum of its parts'. From a series of apparently simple (if disarmingly unusual and original) propositions, Chodzko's work conjures a uniquely altered perspective on the world; oblique, enigmatic, uncanny, yet intimately grounded in familiar surroundings and in recognisable experience. *Plan for a Spell* is exemplary in this – under the (playful, parodic) sign of a cabbala (which is, after all, the method of decoding the language that God passed down to Adam…), what Chodzko is actually proposing is a kind of re-enchantment of a shared social space, a new poetics of the everyday.

This book, published to coincide with the tour of *Plan for a Spell*, features four newly commissioned texts, which range widely across Chodzko's body of work and provide an illuminating insight into the work of one of the most distinctive and inventive voices on the contemporary scene. My thanks go to those four writers, to Mappin Art Gallery in Sheffield (our partners in commissioning *Plan for a Spell*), and, of course, to Adam Chodzko himself.

Steven Bode, Film and Video Umbrella, London, March 2002

'Pay no attention to that man behind the curtain'

Will Bradley

From Beyond | 1996

Artists have a problem, a big problem. They've lost control. Once, maybe, they had a role, mediating somehow between the banal and the sublime, taking on the big issues, gazing into the existential void. But the world caught up and overtook them and then somehow forgot, and the world doesn't want to be reminded. The world wants artists to perform, to entertain. And the artists, in turn, are caught in an impossible trap, paralysed by contradiction, doomed to fail.

Adam Chodzko's work can be seen as a paradoxical study of this problem by the method of avoidance. Like those medieval sects who believed they could only truly be saved once they had experienced every kind of sin, Chodzko is trying to describe the indescribable – the infinite, the sublime – by repeatedly exposing the tricks, self-deceptions and calculated illusions that make up the language he has to use.

Reunion: 'Salò' and *From Beyond* for example, like a lot of Chodzko's works, turn back on themselves twice. By giving a voice and a history to bit-part actors from Pasolini's and Russell's metaphysical epics 'Salò' and 'The Devils', they disrupt the aura of the films and any claim they might have made to spiritual truth. Instead Chodzko's works present the filmmaking process as a lived experience, a significant event in individual lives. They ask us to look at the films in the same way that we look at the artwork that uses them – as associations of people and events guided as much by chance as by intention, and as artefacts whose ultimate meaning or outcome can never be measured or known, whose meaning is distributed and hidden in the lives and experiences both of everyone who saw them and of all those who took part in their making. All of which leads, in a convoluted way, to images which allow the original question of spiritual truth to return – images of people who have been defined to the world at large by a fictional character, by brief moments of almost-fame, but who have since, of course, lived and thought and acted independently of this, and to whom this moment in front of the camera – that paradoxically constitutes everything we know about them – is only one, probably minor, event in that unknowable, uncountable sequence that makes up an individual life.

The people who take part in Chodzko's work are never just symbols. They're never generic faces or bodies, stereotypes or archetypes. They're never characters either, with fixed collections of personality traits or psychological histories that somehow explain their actions. Instead, they're decentred, defined in relation to something or someone else, caught in the constant process of reconstructing their identity. There's always something missing – the mother in *Producing Siblings*, the consummation of a fantasy in *Involva*, consumer satisfaction and a comfortable self-image in *The Most Hated Item of Clothing Convention*, and the Big Guy himself in *The God Look-Alike Contest*. Of course there's no chance of becoming the owner of a cast-iron coherent sense of self because something strange has happened to time, to memory. The past is an image like any other, read in context and subject to unpredictable change. The past turns out to depend on the present and also, most significantly, on the future. Even the *Secretors*, probably the closest to autonomous objects that Chodzko has ever come, don't present themselves as features of the architecture but as features of reality

and its breakdown, erupting not from the everyday fabric of buildings but from somewhere entirely outside of our experience. This investigation of negative space and absent meaning produces as a by-product a large quantity of high-quality and intense pathos, an outcome that is encouraged and manipulated. All these experiences – of the lost, the missing, the forgotten – carry an emotional charge, a calculated trigger for a chain of thought that spins off, away from the work itself, into a wholly subjective world.

Plan for a Spell takes these themes of chance and contingency one stage further. The work reconfigures itself at every viewing, each time asking the viewer whether this particular combination of sound and image could be the promised one, the one with an unnamed power greater than the sum of its parts. The magic of the spell in question is something like the symbolic power of art, presumed missing or lost several centuries ago, and the imagery of the film ranges over ancient traditions and contemporary rituals. In some configurations we even get to see a close-up sequence of basket weaving, possibly the first such instance in the history of video art. It's tempting to see *Plan for a Spell* as a kind of requiem for an unmediated culture, for experiences that haven't been defined to death by their own representation, but there was a time (and that time was the 1970s) when it was possible to find footage like this on mainstream TV. It's more like a simulation of, or a metaphor for, a collective memory. It's an artwork that, with admirable honesty, openly displays its own limitations but also imagines the possibility of transcending them to produce magical effects, encouraging the viewer to speculate on what these effects might be and

Involva (Act I and Act II) | 1995

REUNION

Cerco i ragazzi che sono apparsi nel film *Salò* di Pier Paolo Pasolini (1975).
Seeking the children who appeared in the film *Salò* by Pier Paolo Pasolini (1975).

Olga Andreis, Graziella Aniceto, Benedetta Gaetani, Dorit Henke, Faridah Malik, Giuliana Melis, Renata Moar, Antinisca Nemour, Lamberto Book, Umberto Chessari, Claudio Cicchetti, Gaspare Di Jenno, Sergio Fascetti, Franco Merli, Bruno Musso, Antonio Orlando.

Insieme realizzeremo qualcosa di nuovo.
Together we can create something new.

Per qualunque informazione, contattare Adam Chodzko all'Accademia Britannica:
tel. 06 3230743 (lunedì-venerdì, ore 9.30-17) **fax** 06 3221201
e-mail bsrstu@librs6k.vatlib.it

whether art, now, is really capable of delivering them. Borges wrote that 'the immanence of a revelation that does not occur is, perhaps, the aesthetic phenomenon,' but more than this you get the feeling that the work is a prototype, a proof-of-principle experiment for a much larger and older and more mystical idea. Somewhere in history, in some combination of human knowledge and action, is hidden a greater truth which has either been missed or forgotten – or perhaps more precisely needs to be made, put together from the unreliable and malleable material of experience – but which has the power to transform everything.

I mean, the energy needed for this system to work

Limbo Land could be seen as markedly different to most of Chodzko's previous work, even as it develops many of the same ideas and strategies and again presents itself as incomplete, self-conscious. Long tracking shots showing empty, desolate landscapes from an unearthly, floating viewpoint are intercut with emotionally charged scenes of two people attending the bedside of a third, unseen character. There is a moment when the camera (i.e. the viewer) looks straight into the eyes of the other actors, drawing you into the middle of a scene in which the other characters are also only observers, powerless to influence the outcome. At other times the camera moves through the landscape in ways that don't correspond to any possible human experience of motion, with an intensity that recalls scenes from Tarkovsky's 'Stalker' – a film that was an extended meditation on the meaning of miracles in a secular world. These images are framed by the attempts of a sound recordist to soundtrack the film itself, as she tries to understand what has taken place and how she should respond. So the soundtrack becomes an open, contingent element. We hear it as a

Limbo Land | 2001

"Hi, yes…I just thought I'd tell you that I don't really understand what you want. I couldn't really understand what you meant. Something to do with an ending? Something having gone? The flight of something? So, I'm just imagining how it looks.

And I've just been listening to some sounds, they are suggestions really, some possibilities; stuff I've been collecting. None of them seem to be right at the moment.
I don't know. Maybe I misunderstood something.

I'm listening to the last bits now and then I don't really know what else I can do.
Hope that is OK…..bye."

tentative response to a situation whose meaning is not yet fixed and whose purpose is unclear. At the same time, it guides and alters our experience of watching. Abstract clicks and crackles and echoes drift in space, intensifying the sense of distance, of disconnection, and we realise that this process – the attempt to represent an event that cannot be completely understood or expressed – is the process of the film as a whole.

The bedside vigil, the glimpses of abandoned clothing lying in the snow, the title of the work, all make it clear that this is somehow a representation of the point of transition from life to death. It's also a representation made with the knowledge that it can never be true, or complete – a reflection on the fact that, for all the emotional power of these images, of images in general, certain situations or states of mind are unfilmable, inexpressible. It's a given thing in our society that there are certain questions that are not acceptable to ask. *Limbo Land* is mature enough not to ask these questions directly, but it's intensely concerned with how they might be represented in a meaningful way. In a society where the meaning of death has been allocated to a series of mostly banal categories, *Limbo Land* introduces the idea that we are no nearer to understanding what it is we're talking about, never mind construct a coherent moral or aesthetic system in which it might be expressed.

Chodzko relies on the viewer to create rather than decipher the meaning of his work, but in a fundamentally different way from the way that most classic 'conceptual art' operates. The art itself is not simply a concept; it has a real, sensual existence. It's usually either a real event that people took part in or even, in the case of *Limbo Land*, a wholly fictional scenario that needs to be understood, at least initially, according to well-established codes. It often invokes the currently unfashionable concept of imagination as one of its central ideas. This might seem like an academic distinction, but it isn't. The procedures of conceptual art require that the art as pure idea be enough to communicate the meaning of the work. In Chodzko's situation this is no longer sufficient. The work most often starts with an open-ended question, even a material, political question, which can never be answered in its own terms; a question, sometimes apparently naïve, that can't be answered without stepping outside the framework that makes it possible to ask at all. The work defines an absence of meaning that can only be filled, subjectively, by the person looking at it, in full knowledge of the fact that the predictable, banal answer has already been anticipated and cancelled by the work itself. In Chodzko's art, truth and meaning are mutable, personal ideas. More than that, the work seems to suggest that if the sublime, the infinite, is inexpressible, then our only contact with it can be through our own imagination. It all comes down to personal experience, but that experience turns out to be the most real thing we have.

Sound for "Limbo Land"

Dat c ; 60 minutes.

1m 32 — 8m 55s.
2m 40s — 2m 43s.

2m 27 secs; hum from plumbing and trickle in pipes
✗ 2m 43 secs- 2m 58 secs; reversed Japanese tannoy
6m 42 secs; into cafe; someone singing; people talking — appears to worsen in volume but doesn't.
✓ 8m 46 secs; chimes in background, tv programme; how to make tortillas,..voices too
9m 33 secs; music in background but no talking
9m 54 secs; chimes, spanish voices,...laughter; "he only left 2 weeks" ✗
✗ 11m 16 secs; breathing crickets; walking on dust track
11m 32secs; quiet 'wow',...plane,...walking in dust
11m 39 secs- 12m 25 secs; low pass Melvin Bliss,... humming/singing along, pottering around, sound of Italian sound recording in background No!
✗ 12m 39 secs- 13m 09 secs same as above but song ends.
✗ 19m 40 secs- 20m 10 secs; Seth breathing and fabric sounds
23m 29 secs; kids toy says " Quiet please!" "a one and a 2 and a 3" ✗
29m 49 secs; kids toy says " Yeah alright!" "a one and a 2 and a 3" etc + voices in background; ✓
✗ 28m 41 secs to 29m 50 secs;   people laugh on tv, I laugh; loud cough; cartoon on tv;
✓ 30 m 47 secs; cartoon and bed sounds until 31m 16 secs

REVERSED TANNOY → TRUCK RADIO ‖ MICROLIGHT.

+ Herbert:
phone call in " never give up"
Break in "So Now"
v. end of " we go wrong"

RADIO IN TRUCK / TRUCK SOUND   BREATH / SPACE OF BEDROOM

REVERSED TANNOY

20 secs

MICROLIGHT   REVERSED TANNOY

library atmos.

Sound sample notes for *Limbo Land*

Meetings

Polly Staple

For the past few years Adam Chodzko has been working on a series of drawings entitled *Meeting*; there are now fifteen in total. The A2 drawings follow the format of a poster. In a neat sans serif font they announce 'Meeting of people with stammers to describe a fire. Here. Everyone welcome'. This statement frames an intricate ink drawing of agile lines and arrows which from a distance does indeed resemble a fire; the lines curl and intermesh like flames, but up close they are an arrangement of very precise marks. The edge of the paper is bordered by a fluorescent orange pigment. The format of the poster is the same for each drawing but the crazy bundle of marks signifying 'fire' alters – you could even say stammers – from poster to poster.

The *Meeting* drawings seem to contain the essence of Chodzko's project as an artist. They are very beautiful, aesthetically and conceptually precise, yet testing the limits of something which is ultimately wholly intangible. The pictures comment on the viewer's desire to make sense of, to 'read', an artwork and locate meaning within the image. The poster's statement invokes the voice of authority; telling you a fact, imparting information. The statement is all-inclusive: everyone's welcome. It all seems disarmingly simple: there's a meeting and here's a picture of a fire for you to discuss. But just at the point that you weigh up the announcement and begin to evaluate the information, your train of thought is upset and disrupted. A meeting of stammerers would be ludicrous at the best of times, but to describe a fire..!

If it's hard to rationalise how and why *Meeting* actually works, it's easier to appreciate its singular effect. The piece hits you straight between the eyes: a very complex one-liner. The posters utilise a system running on its own steam; the seriality – or rather the suggestion of infinite variation within seriality – summoning a very pleasurable excess of information. Chodzko's *Meeting* drawings have something in common with his new piece *Plan for a Spell*; and not only because they both flirt with images of fire and witchcraft. The whole idea of planning a spell, like the idea of organising a meeting of stammerers, is typically Chodzko, in that it sounds deceptively logical, but doesn't quite add up. Two plus two in Chodzko's work always equals five.

Chodzko has made a number of works utilising the strategy of placing an advertisement in the free ads paper 'Loot' to varying degrees of effect. *The International God Look-Alike Contest* consists of the assemblage by Chodzko of images sent in by those responding to a search for 'people who think they look like God'. And who knows what the response to the insertion of 'Millenarian heterogeneous apparition, 3 metres, unstructured model, reasonable condition...' in the 'Scientific Equipment' section of 'Loot' on 17th March 1993 could possibly be? *Inverter (Clearance Sale)* signals an equally subtle but more materialistically orientated enquiry into how we may structure our everyday universe. *Inverter (Clearance Sale)* consists of page 105 from the November 1998 issue of 'Harpers & Queen' displaying an advertisement for 'Adler' jewellery accompanied by three co-relating adverts placed by Chodzko in 'Loot'. The 'Adler' page depicts the image of a woman in an evening gown in anonymous wetlands; there's a bird in the distance and the woman holds her arm outstretched proffering an ineptly photo-shopped image of a diamond necklace. The evocative

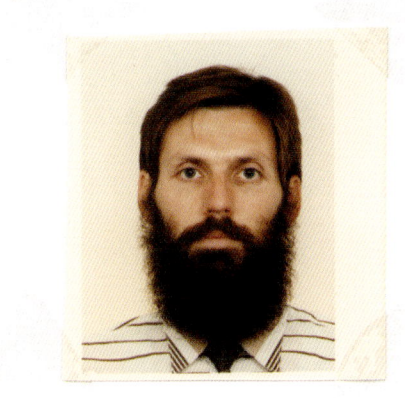

The International God Look-Alike Contest | 1995/96

strap-line states: 'Memoires de Femmes, Memoires du Monde' with a footnote informing one that this is 'Ruya: an ample and generous white gold necklace gracefully adorned with one thousand, five hundred and twenty eight diamonds... This necklace is a unique piece.'

Chodzko's 'Loot' placements utilise a very different language and ordering system. One, circled in red felt tip pen in the 'Collecting and Hobbies' section, is for a 'Wing, made of metal and broken glass (1m long). Only one of a pair. Strange fancy costume. £30 ono... No time wasters please.' Chodzko's no-nonsense description punctures the pomposity of the 'Adler' ad – fabricating a convoluted desiring system with imaginary plenitude and by the simplest of means. 'Harpers and Queen' is full of advertisements for luxury goods accompanied by socially aspirational editorial. Setting out a fiercely hierarchical social order, the magazine's power spins on the allure of symbolic exchange. Chodzko's adverts offer both a humorous commentary on this system but more importantly invert this system, inserting it into another more democratic yet still materially orientated world in which all the enhancing embellishment of money and status is stripped away to be replaced by a different sense of value. Chodzko also subverts a physical sense of scale. Here the entire structure of the picture is completely misunderstood as if the copywriter came from another planet. A sea bird and its reflection are misinterpreted as a 'stuffed sepia coloured Double Duck. Ornamental' and its size is perceived as 'actual', therefore tiny.

In *Plan for a Spell* Chodzko develops his investigation of rational and irrational structures and how 'things'

may come together; here he is reliant on a DVD player which randomly shuffles the images and texts that have been programmed onto a DVD disk into an entirely arbitrary sequence. *Plan for a Spell* consists of an assemblage of visual segments, soundtracks and textual overlays in different configurations triggered by this random playing. One may encounter a clear, close-up shot of a man's hands basket weaving. The soundtrack however – noisy shouting from a crowd – does not match the considered rhythm of the man's dexterously moving hands. The basket weaving cuts to footage of the charred remains of a funeral pyre of burning cattle set within a picturesque landscape; this segues into a scrummage of people chasing after each other, pursuing something. There's an atmospheric musical soundtrack which again transforms into the soporific whirr and hum of wind turbines, the sound then coinciding with a close-up of the turbines themselves. The faint, almost inaudible murmur of the man basket weaving suddenly appears over footage of an urban street; crowds pass by and cars whizz past but the sound (and mood) of the basket weaving blends disconcertingly into this new footage. 'About 10 minutes ago, didn't it feel better?' Suddenly there is an entirely new sequence: deadpan footage of trees overlaid by a televisual grid; a cinematic pan across a skyline at dusk; another cinematic shot of a gigantic burning wicker man; stock-car racing; a crowd charging around with a fire barrel; the sweeping overview of computer-generated houses lining a computer-generated street; a real man dressed in a burr costume draped in a Scottish flag being paraded down a small-town street...

The informal subtitles comment on, confuse and complement the seemingly haphazard yet meticulously constructed combination of images. The written word and the visual image implode determined by their dialogical relationship within a continuously evolving system. Strangely, the subtitles have the effect of spoken language; as if you are in conversation with the narrator, sharing some multiplicitous secret. A persistent yet seductively unfathomable logic keeps you in play. There is magic here.

Chodzko's terrain seems peculiarly English but modulated, and manipulated, by a distinctly un-English intellectualism. There is the polite stammering Englishman of *Meeting*; the very particular snobbery of 'Harpers' and the no-nonsense DIY aesthetic of 'Loot'. This is combined with the historical lyricism of the English pagan pastoral set out in *Plan for a Spell*, the cultural specifics of foot and mouth, the new ecology of wind turbines and modern leisure activities set against a backdrop of folk rituals. The social spaces encountered in *Plan for a Spell* are very different from those outlined in *Inverter (Clearance Sale)* but are not unconnected. If you live in a city you may desire the countryside. If you live in a city you may find the rural bizarre but be attracted to an idea of the pastoral. How it might be possible to attain a sense of community within either environment is more problematic. The 21st century city has been colonised by the homogenising spirit of middle England and it may be that the countryside now offers the free space for cultural experimentation that the city used to offer. The flow of capital has meant that cities like London have become havens for 1980s out-of-towners and American imports; for those who have settled, drink coffee at Starbucks and think they are in 'Friends'. This is complicated but we are made of complex stuff.

Chodzko is both a fabricator and a flâneur of these different spaces; idler, wanderer, wonderer, director, producer... he takes the unexpected turn (which is usually, unerringly, the right turn) and we collide.

It is noteworthy that Chodzko made *Inverter (Clearance Sale)* in 1999, at a time when London – where Chodzko then lived – was enjoying a social and economic boom. Perspectives (and commodities) were shifting with all the crassness that Cool Britannia/BritPop/BritArt could muster. There's a strange vacuum now. We're all Modern but no one's quite sure what Contemporary means; we desire something more, something else, another dimension. Chodzko now lives in Whitstable in Kent; in the countryside, near the sea. Considering the territory of *A Plan for a Spell* this seems important. Chodzko holds a funny position in the art world: he often acts as a facilitator or curator but he is not interested in curating artists; he organises small rallies and social gatherings but he is not concerned with the clichéd and overtly literal limitations of 'socially engaged practice'; he makes art infused with the language of cinema but pertaining to the non-sequential order of the imagination, encountered as installations rather than narrative documents. He is of the 'yBa' generation but he has more in common with the subversive strategies of 1960s conceptual artists such as Douglas Huebler than with the spectacular bombast of Damien Hirst. Chodzko's art is difficult to categorise. This is one of his strengths; utilising the margins for good effect; he's always shifting the goal posts, nimble-footed, pursuing his own path.

In all his work Chodzko assumes the role of the director-magician and seems to position the viewer as code-breaker. As a matter of habit, human beings look for patterns in what they see, for linear relations and fixed points. However if there is no linearity, searching for deterministic rules within a system becomes both frustrating and exhilaratingly unpredictable. Chodzko utilises an image of the crowd which is unstable and aperiodic; he facilitates situations in which people come together for specific reasons to exchange information but with unforeseeable results; he explores the subtle relations between simplicity and complexity, orderliness and randomness and the connections in between. What strikes me most is the precision of the 'content' – practical, social or imaginary – set against this more disruptive 'form'. Chodzko doesn't so much invent his own language as an artist but invents his own system, his own way of dealing with the world, filtered through a very particular set of variables and then bounced back, but now somewhat altered, somewhat odd. Chodzko posits a landscape that clearly recognises factual reality seemingly made up of the things that surround us, but it is entirely a fiction; a free territory determined by a very generous imagination.

Plan for a Spell

is directly generated by these movements.

This motion is really good.

So, I can see there must be

something special about this too.

Is it too chaotic?

Now that everything seems out of alignment?

Portrait of the Artist as a Dust Wrangler

Chris Darke

'Without the images of drama, adventure, comedy, natural and artificial events imprinted on motion picture film there would be no cinema: there would be nothing to make history out of: filmology would have nowhere to go. In its place would be either still images (photography) or fleeting ones (electronics). The point is confirmed by video: a civilization that is prey to the nightmare of its visual memory has no further need of cinema. For cinema is the art of destroying moving images.'

Paolo Cherchi Usai 'The Death of Cinema: History, Cultural Memory and the Digital Dark Age'

In April 1996 Adam Chodzko placed a classified advertisement in the London listings paper 'Loot' that ran: 'Film Dust from 'Walkabout', 'The Railway Children', 'Logan's Run', photo of Jenny Agutter, unsigned, also glass eyeballs, any offers.' What could one possibly offer in exchange for a treasure such as 'film dust'? And where could such dust have been gathered? From the locations of the films themselves? From the decayed matter of the films' celluloid reels? From cinemas where the films were once projected through the 'glass eyeball' of the lens? Or was it a residue of 'stardust' extracted from the heavenly form of Jenny Agutter that Chodzko wanted to shift? I've dutifully checked film credits ever since seeing Chodzko's advertisement but, among all the 'Gaffers' and 'Best Boys', I've yet to come across a credit for 'Dust Wrangler'.

Chodzko's 'dust wrangling' activities continue. In the overlooked corners of cinema's past he has unearthed and reanimated extras from films as disparate as Pasolini's 'Salò', Ken Russell's 'The Devils' and Fellini's 'City of Women'. Such reanimation yielded its own splendid serendipity in the case of Chodzko's *Reunion: 'Salò'*. When he advertised in Italy for the actors who played the degraded and murdered children in Pier Paolo Pasolini's 'Salò or 120 Days of Sodom' (1975), the only member of the original cast to come forward was a woman who had declined to act out her own death during the shoot (Chodzko had to find 'doubles' to play the missing extras). Less a version of the 'remake' popular among some artists vis-a-vis classic films, Chodzko's approach saw cinema as providing both a 'vanishing point' (into which the extras disappear) and a 'horizon' of possible events (precisely, to locate such extras and restore them to life). That's to say, cinema has provided Chodzko with both the material and the method by which to pursue his artistic project (one that cannot be defined solely by its interest in film and the moving image, it should be said). Because cinema, even when remembered (especially when remembered), provides an instant community between two people who remember the same film. Any divergence of individual memories or disagreements over favourite moments simply enhances this communion. Chodzko has set about exploring the possibility of producing work from just such a shared set of references. Sometimes that memory is very specific, almost canonical (if more than a little 'cursed'), as in the case of 'Salò'. But it needn't be so to function effectively. In *A Place for 'The End'* Chodzko asked eight local people to each select locations around Birmingham that could serve as settings for the final frame of an imaginary film. At each site a generic ending was filmed showing these 'locations people' leaving the shot and 'entering' the backgrounds of the places they had chosen. The resulting images were dictated by these participants, as is often the case with

Reunion; *Salò* | 1998

A Place for *The End* | 1999

Chodzko's work. *A Place for 'The End'* was also about the act of 'framing'. How to 'frame' a commonplace local vista to give it the sense of dramatic finality and nearly mythical resonance that the final shot of a film should ideally possess? How to make the off-screen space pregnant with event? And how to 'frame' under the thoroughly internalised influence of cinema's widescreen rectangle? From this procedure came a psycho-geographical mapping of Birmingham according not so much to cinema's image-repertoire as to its edges. Again, the sense of 'vanishing-points' and 'event-horizons' were strongly present in the video and photographic installation that the project generated.

Chodzko is not alone in his fascination with the cinema. Since the early 1990s it has become evident that cinema has been the key medium of reference for many contemporary artists. The pace and range of this art-film engagement has become so intense and widespread that it's possible, even at this early stage, to identify some emerging tendencies. For example, at the Tate International Conference 'Moving Image as Art: Time-Based Media in the Gallery' held in London in June 2001, the American curator William Horrigan asked the question: 'At what point did we stop referring to 'video-art'?' The answer being, when 'video-art' started to look like 'cinema'; when it started to be shown in darkened rooms, sometimes equipped with seats, and was projected at the scale of a cinema screen rather than a television monitor. What Horrigan referred to as the 'dominance of projection' seemed to indicate a generational divide between those involved in single-screen monitor-based video and those working with the possibilities of projection which digital technologies enable. Another contributor to the Tate event, David Hall, a pioneer of artists' video in the UK and credited with the introduction of the term 'time-based media', made the distinction clear. In 1970s video-art, the audience were seen as 'collaborators' in the work whose presence was required to 'complete' it. With projected video, the audience become observers of a quasi-cinematic 'spectacle'. The implication here is an old one: that the 'spectacle' that comes with the scale of such projection renders the viewer 'passive'.

There's little doubt, however, that the now widespread availability of digital projection technology has played a major part in the rise of the quasi-cinematic 'spectacle' in gallery spaces. Two features immediately follow, both of which are treated in Chodzko's most recent piece, *Plan for a Spell*: 1) the possibility of an almost endless looping of images that comes with digital data storage capacities; 2) the possibility for multiple screen projections. So, the spatial considerations of scale are attended simultaneously by considerations of time, with the possibility of an 'impossible' duration, an 'eternal' temporality, in which projection might take place. Both of these elements – scale and duration, space and time – provide ways to examine the staging of the projection-event as it occurs in the gallery environment. Multiple projection maximises the quality of 'spectacle' while stretching and fragmenting the temporal frame across several fields simultaneously. A kind of 'montage in three dimensions' takes place. This form of projection event, even with its many variations, has become a commonplace presence in the gallery. But to define what sets *Plan for a Spell* apart from this orthodoxy requires first that we examine how Chodzko presents his images.

And what images they are. To these metropolitan eyes, Chodzko has assembled a compendium of rural arcana: tar barrelling from Devon, the Burry Man from Scotland, and from Cumbria a host of sequences including wicker weaving, wind turbines, a demolition derby, pyres of cattle cadavers (slaughtered during the foot and mouth outbreak) and a huge scrum of men that lurches, scatters and regroups as it careers up hill and down dale. These images have the unemphatic force of documentary material. The framing is generally unassertive, keyed to motion, action and significant detail. This material, not quite 'raw', is not yet 'shaped'. And that's where the projection-event that Chodzko has developed for *Plan for a Spell* comes in. The sequences rewind at random in single-screen projection, as though the hand of some invisible editor is worrying them into new combinations. Some images mutate from within. A camera pans across a wooded horizon that it reads like an audio line, a verdant radio-dial. The sound is strange: a plucked string, a resonating glissando mixed with noises that might be heard coming from the radio in the room above. Sound, only occasionally illustrating the image, often seems to come from another space unconnected to the images themselves. The work is making itself as we watch. The elements here are radically separate; on the vertical level of image and sound as well as on the horizontal level of montage, of the sequences themselves. Nothing gells into any kind of recognisable continuity. This work is radically out of synch with itself.

A further feature compounds this impression: the subtitles that run beneath the clusters of images. In cinema, subtitles usually signify translation, the presence of a foreign language. Here they signify differently. The subtitled commentary has a rhetorical function relative to the images. That's to say, it makes them provisional. The subtitles refer to 'structures' and 'patterns' visible in the filmed sequences. It insists on the generational power of 'movement' and 'collisions' within and between such sequences, and highlights the desire to identify meaning as both 'made' and 'unmade' in the same mo(ve)ment. From the collisions of cars in the demolition derby footage, or the surging and scattering movements of the scrumming bodies, it becomes clear that, as well as being documents, these images are also declarations of the work's process. Like Godard's famous shots of the cosmos in a coffee-cup from 'Deux ou trois choses que je sais d'elle' (1966), they are the image and its analysis at the same time. Like Godard, Chodzko wants to 'show' and 'show himself showing'. Consider the register of the subtitling, its hesitancy of tone, its tentativeness in identifying an image as 'this thing' or 'that fact'. Observe how the subtitles will say, at one moment, 'So, this is nothing, I'm sure,' only to instantly qualify this statement by adding 'but that's probably why it's important.' What we can identify here, and throughout the subtitling, is the rhetorical device of deferred narration. The object of Chodzko's narrative is to ask 'when' and 'where' to start speaking about the images, and not yet (not ever?) to speak of what the images are, to describe them. It is a rhetoric that is at least one step removed from that upon which it comments, that has not yet found a language it trusts to fit, to 'complete' and to 'fix' the images. I am able to identify two of the rhetorical figures that Chodzko employs in *Plan*. One of these is called 'merismus', the dividing of a whole into its parts. The other is 'enumeratio', the division of a subject into its adjuncts, a cause into its effects.

Plan for a Spell | 2001

SUBTITLES

[33 - 36 secs] So, some kind of structure is being made,
[36 - 38 secs] although I suppose it doesn't yet look
[38 - 41 secs] like it's becoming anything in particular.
[55 - 58 secs] It's good though just to look for a pattern.

[30 - 32 secs] This must be included because
[32 - 35 secs] there is something hard and unstable about it.
[35 - 38 secs] And fragile too.
[40 - 42 secs] Maybe not in the movement
[42 - 44 secs] which seems so blocked
[44 - 47 secs] and interrupted by these collisions
[49 - 52 secs] but there is something…
[56 - 58 secs] So, what next?

[9 - 12 secs] This is better;
[12 - 14 secs] now we're getting somewhere.
[18 - 21 secs] I don't know how to begin to describe this one
[21 - 24 secs] because, this is all preparation,
[24 - 26 secs] a kind of dressing,
[26 - 29 secs] at the same time making and unmaking.
[35 - 38 secs] But it seems very different now.
[38 - 42 secs] Something has shifted.

[5 - 7 secs] So, this is nothing, I'm sure,
[7 - 9 secs] but that's probably why it's important
[9 - 12 secs] to leave it in.
[15 - 18 secs] These are props.
[18 - 21 secs] I mean, both that they took part in a fiction
[21 - 24 secs] but also supported a structure in that fiction.
[24 - 28 secs] So, now they act as links between us
[28 - 31 secs] and a story about what we could be.
[57 - 59 secs] Ok… let's move on.

[5 - 8 secs] Maybe this is a good place to start from
[8 - 11 secs] I mean, the energy needed for this system to work
[11 - 14 secs] is directly generated by these movements.
[45 - 48 secs] This motion is really good.

[10 - 13 secs] So, I can see there must be
[13 - 16 secs] something special about this too.
[28 - 31 secs] Is it too chaotic?
[31 - 34 secs] Now that everything seems out of alignment?
[48 - 51 secs] I guess it may all be much simpler than it appears.

[1 - 2 secs] In comes another.
[4 - 7 secs] This immediately feels darker,
[7 - 9 secs] but it might be placed exactly here
[9 - 12 secs] for balance.
[15 - 17 secs] It seems naff calling it a 'spell'
[17 - 19 secs] but let's be sure of something at least;

[19 - 22 secs] the programming of this is using magic
[22 - 24 secs] (again, sounds a bit dodgy)
[24 - 26 secs] but when the spell encoded within it
[26 - 28 secs] reaches the right combination
[28 - 31 secs] you'll feel different;
[31 - 34 secs] distinctly clearer for an instant.
[36 - 38 secs] I'm not sure in what way exactly,
[38 - 40 secs] probably the effect is pretty subtle;
[40 - 43 secs] maybe like a pressure lifting.
[45 - 48 secs] But it's somewhere in the transitions,
[48 - 51 secs] in how things coincide and assemble.
[54 - 56 secs] Everything is running randomly, so
[56 - 58 secs] at some point, I've no idea when,
[58 - 60 secs] the right configuration is reached.

[14 - 16 secs] So, not this bit. Not yet.
[16 - 19 secs] we'll reach it soon though, I think,
[19 - 21 secs] the thing that needs including.
[29 - 31 secs] Not what you see here
[31 - 34 secs] but only what is viewed from this point
[34 - 37 secs] exactly here;
[41 - 42 secs] (sometimes it's very specific).

[6 - 9 secs] This is quite nice
[9 - 12 secs] but I'm not sure how it relates at the moment.
[15 - 18 secs] OK, the sound generated right here must also
[18 - 21 secs] be a vital part of making it work.
[54 - 57 secs] Maybe you're noticing some changes by now,
[57 - 60 secs] I guess it depends what comes next.

[1 - 3 secs] So this next?
[3 - 5 secs] But maybe this is not so important.
[15 - 17 secs] What we're looking for here is a shift that
[17 - 20 secs] happens when there is a change in the light,
[20 - 23 secs] when a shadow passes across us.
[27 - 30 secs] But there's something else too.
[33 - 36 secs] Soon, you'll see the same movement
[36 - 39 secs] shared by two people simultaneously.
[42 - 45 secs] Actually, that's not so amazing in itself
[45 - 47 secs] but it echoes something elsewhere.
[52 - 55 secs] About 10 minutes ago,
[55 - 58 secs] didn't it feel better?

[5 - 7 secs] So, now it has to find somewhere else
[7 - 10 secs] to try other combinations.
[10 - 12 secs] It might have reached the right sequence
[12 - 14 secs] already, it's kind of difficult to tell
[14 - 17 secs] when it can't stop making itself.
[20 - 23 secs] Maybe it needs more time…
[23 - 25 secs] or maybe some distance.
[25 - 27 secs] I mean, for the spell to work
[27 - 30 secs] it might be better to forget about it.

What is unusual about *Plan for a Spell* is the layered attention given to montage at the lateral level. It's not montage as weaving together but as separation. Hence the term 'montage' which I use to invoke a tradition of deconstructive editing that goes all the way back to Eisenstein and Vertov, that extends through the work of Godard and Marker and that is always associated with the 'other cinema' that has existed fitfully alongside its narrative counterpart. It seems entirely fitting that *Plan for a Spell* should take on this feature of film-making. The canonical example of what André Bazin described as 'lateral' editing is Chris Marker's 1958 film 'Lettre de Sibérie'. Marker presents a set of images shot in what was then the Soviet Republic of Yakutsk. Firstly, the commentary informs us that the images are of 'a modern city… comfortable buses… happy Soviet workers.' Secondly, we are told Yakutsk is 'a dusky city of sombre repute' in which 'the potentates of the regime flaunt [their] insolent luxury' and where the workers are 'hunched over like slaves.' Finally, the same images represent 'modern houses gradually replacing the sombre old quarters' where the workers 'apply themselves to beautifying their city, which is in need of it.' From Soviet propaganda to anti-Soviet misinformation via an equally misleading 'neutrality' of tone, each commentary contradicts the other while the images obdurately remain the same, neither confirming nor denying the truth of Marker's comically competing voice-overs.

It seems fitting to use Marker as an example because he (like Godard, but to a slightly more limited extent) is one of the few undisputed modernist masters who has worked with multimedia formats (electronic images and CD Rom) as well with installations. *Plan for a Spell* announces the possibility of revitalising, in another context, the technique of 'lateral montage'. This opens the gallery-projection to interpretation via cinema history while avoiding it being seen as a purely 'spectacular' and quasi-'cinematic' projection-event. In the very process of 'separating the elements', film and art join hands again.

When Chodzko invented the craft of 'dust wrangling' he can only have guessed at how many others were out there among the film-going public, shoring up and restoring in the archives and film museums, rummaging among Super-8 reels at car-boot sales, digging deep into bins of gash-tape. But he may well have remarked on the new wave of dust-wranglers who were at work in the gallery, fashioning cinematic forms of their own from the same dust that Chodzko once offered for sale.

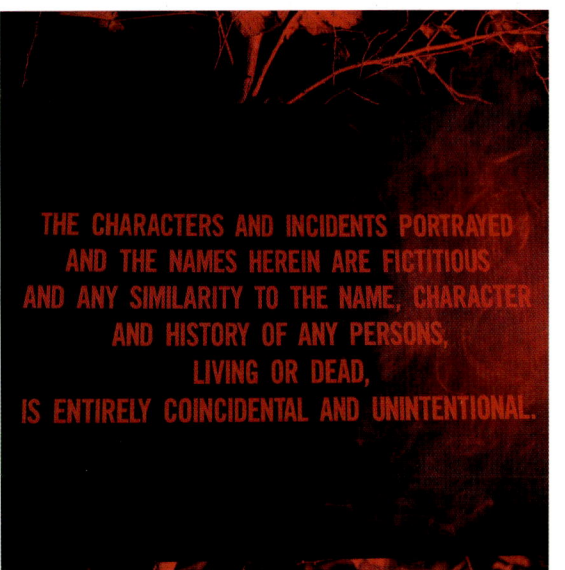

"Loose Disclaimer"

Dispersed on the ends of the following video tapes:

(1) "Black Narcissus," (Powell/Pressburger), video store, Soho, London.

(2) "The Player," (Robert Altman), video store, Ambleside, Cumbria.

(3) "Shivers," (David Cronenburg), video store, Sheffield.

(4) "The Barefoot Kid," (Johnny To), video store, Brixton, London.

(5) "Fearless," (Peter Weir), video store, Bedford Avenue, Brooklyn, USA.

(6) "Where the Green Ants Dream," (Werner Herzog), video store, Sheffield.

Better Scenery | 2000

Better Scenery | 2001

Better Scenery

Head south out of Ambleside, Cumbria, to the Grizedale Visitor Centre. From whichever car park you arrive in find your way to the entrance to the shop. From here face south-west and follow the red banded posts out of the walled garden. Once through the green door in the wall turn right and follow the road to Home Farm. Arriving at the farmhouse turn left through the gate into the field. Make sure you close that gate! Walk (or cycle) uphill on the forest track through the meadow, past the cattle grid to the road. Take a left turn and head south through the ancient oak woods. The track through Hall Wood passes fields on the left. 1.5 km further on from the cattle grid facing west (to your right) is a carpet of bilberry bushes beneath oak trees with a stream running down towards the left.

Situated here, in this place, is a sign which describes the location of this sign you have just finished reading.

Hinterland

Jeremy Millar

The van skates lazily around the roundabout, around us; in its wing mirror, floating against the bare banks and concrete flyovers, a face swollen with swearing. Welcome, it seems to be saying; you're welcome to it.

The island seems a very different place, but then islands often do: self-contained, bounded (I can hardly say insular). We have decided to walk along around its south-eastern corner, the exact area visible from our shore on the mainland, taking some photographs, perhaps, and talking about Adam's work. It seems appropriate, given that so much of it seems concerned with the description of place, and the rituals that might make up that description. At the side of the road, as we approach the bridge, lies a mass of blood and fur – a badger, or a boar even? It seems to mark a place where the memory of a journey begins, Adam says, mnemonics being made more vivid by the liberal splashing of blood. I bear this in mind as I peer forward into my wing mirror.

Approaching the roundabout, we notice that the junction to the right leads to the prisons, so we decide to visit there first. A flag hangs halfway down the pole outside the fire station; a burned-out house opposite persists like a dark rumour behind a thicket of bushes and trees. We pass a number of different buildings, and areas for parking, and follow as the road slides straight ahead, and down into a view of the sewage works and marshes below. At the top of a grass bank on the left hand side, its position seemingly arbitrary, a circular road sign proclaims 'OUT OF BOUNDS', though there are no bounds to see except, perhaps, the darkening and dissolving shadow cast by the sign itself. We stop the car and take a photograph. It is the last frame on my roll and so I begin to replace it, dropping the exposed roll into my pocket. I fiddle with the spools as a security guard walks towards us. We give him our names, where we're from, and no we didn't realise that we were on Home Office property. Was there a sign? Oh, we must have missed it. I imagine Adam's registration number being checked at the gatehouse and telling its own story. 'So, why were you taking photographs of the buildings?' I look at Adam. 'We like prison architecture... Where d'you think we could get some slides?' he says, hoping this approach will discourage further interest.

The sun lights the unlit signs above the washboard-shuttered shopfronts, but not all of the amusement arcades are closed. A couple of them seem barely awake, grumbling onto the street like a bad riser needing their first cigarette. We park the car around the corner, next to a pitch of wasteground; a mass of concrete slabs (walls? ceilings? floors?) jagged at its centre, behind it a crushed can caravan. Two men park just behind us and watch as we get out and walk towards the arcades. A short section of Jean Michel Jarre's 'Oxygene' echoes across the road, three versions actually, phased from one another, each separated by the second or two it would take to switch each machine on. It seems an appropriate soundtrack to this place, its theme tune, caught somewhere between an inescapable past and the escapes of the future, and destined to play itself out like this, again and again, day after day.

We walk past the 'Talk of the Town Fun Pub', past the seaside flotsam of aluminium barrels and plastic wash baskets, cushions and carpet washed up against its

back wall, and into a small area of residential maisonettes. Flat-roofed and balconied, they have a vaguely Iberian feel to them, as though drawn up by a municipal architect after a particularly traumatic holiday. The council's money had obviously run out before they surfaced the road. A large community hall stands empty to one side of the residencies, occupying a fenced-in section of land directly by the sea. It is extraordinary. Someone has placed colour photocopies in the windows, like a section from an encyclopaedia, showing the bombs that dropped here, or a liner which sailed from here, or even a photograph of Westminster Bridge from the turn of the century ('Look no cars' it points out, helpfully). In the next window, a herd of toy dinosaurs roam around the spider plants. In the yard at the front, someone has planted plastic flowers in the borders.

We continue further down the coast, past the holiday villages and along the shoreline. The road deteriorates badly – at first A and then B, we had now come to the end of the short highway alphabet – and we swerve and swoop down and around the craters in its surface. We slow, then stop further down the road, in a grassy lay-by marked by a bin, plastic rubbish bags and a pink and blue divan. On the other side of the bank, a boat is berthed on a wooden cradle at the top of the beach, reluctant to enter the water it looks out upon. Its windows are boarded over; it has a suburban front door. Adam walks off up the beach, taking photographs, while I hold back, watching the man in one of the beach houses watching Adam through binoculars. I wonder what stories, what fantasies of paranoia or vengeance are being projected through those lenses into the dark space of his mind (probably none worse than those we attribute to him as we walk back past his dark windows minutes later). Further down, the district council sign informs us that 'CLOTHING MUST BE WORN BEYOND THIS POINT.' Some birds take off behind us.

The path is about the width of the drainage ditch beside it, the one mirroring the other. As though prompted by our presence, the water splits suddenly through the cushion of grass on the bank and spills across the earth just before us, as though they might change places, that the water might once more take control (if it had ever relinquished it completely). Round the curve at the end, we reach the beach – made, it seems, almost entirely of oyster shells, like scaled-up scales – and make our way towards the concrete lookout post. Across the marsh, water and grasses, thick blues and yellows, look like a bad old bruise. Nearby, huge chunks of wood lie amongst more concrete wreckage, and the frayed nerves of steel rope twisted from the ground. The concrete structure is low and angular, its corners cut off, with a slightly more elevated lookout position rising from its roof. Small black holes punctuate the grey-brown walls, a slice having been taken from the corner that looks out over the brown-grey water to our town. It is alien and appropriate and sadly beautiful. I walk around the structure and approach the empty corner that marks its entrance, Adam watching me. The walls lead one way and then another, now trapping light from its interior as it was once designed to trap incoming shells. I wonder what I might find in there, who might be found in there, who might have found themselves in there. How safe are these outposts of security, and is sanctuary always to be found within its thick sound-swallowing walls?

Inside is not so bad; no piss-streaked walls, no porn, no condoms, no needles. A couple of beer cans and 'THUG LIFE' sprayed onto one of the walls. Relief, and perhaps a little disappointment.

The tide seems to be coming in much faster now. The beach has set into waves of its own along which we walk, sliding down its weed-flecked crests. The sound of shell washing against shell, delicate and all around us. We stay there for some time, unable to leave, held like the water as it enters the drift of reeds, slowing, thickening, transformed.

Below the path, to the south, the bends of streams add a fearfully grinning mouth to eyes excavated from the marshland. Perhaps the faces are deliberate, the portrayal of malevolent spirits living within this strange in-between world. Perhaps they are part of some local ritual. 'The faces on Jammy Dodgers are exactly based on these,' Adam says, with a certain irrefutable authority.

The bird watchers' hide has been visible for some time, a point on the landscape to which we are drawn, and around which the landscape is drawn, like the lookout earlier on. I think of a poem – Wallace Stevens' 'Anecdote of the Jar' – which had been read out during a symposium on Robert Smithson at which Adam and myself had both spoken. The poem begins:

I placed a jar in Tennessee,
And round it was, upon a hill.
It made the slovenly wilderness
Surround that hill.

This immediately feels darker,

The jar becomes a point of focus for the surrounding landscape, a point of closure, perhaps, a point of entry in a vast open space. Adam comments on some pieces of litter lying at the side of the path. Perhaps this is less laziness, or a lack of care, than a simple desire to mark the landscape, to determine one's own presence within it. I think of Lawrence Weiner setting off a firework to mark a boundary, a sign no different in some ways from the one the Home Office had erected and which we had used to mark our first stop and first photograph. A choice both deliberate and yet somewhat arbitrary, which is probably just another way of saying 'history'.

Perhaps it is the thought of fireworks, perhaps it is this watery place, but we begin to talk about Peter Greenaway's film 'Drowning by Numbers'. The boy, Smut, sets off a firework to celebrate each violent death he comes across in the countryside, a marking of something which is at once ordinary and extraordinary; which death is, of course, perhaps even more so than life. It is a game, of sorts, a ritual, by which the world and its uncertainties are held within some sort of framework, and if the framework can be known and to some extent predicted, then the world can be also. He is not the only one: the film begins with a girl skipping, and with each revolution of her rope another star is named and added to her collection, up to the number 100 – 'A hundred is enough. Once you've counted a hundred, all the other hundreds are the same.' Yet even knowing the stars so well, she cannot foresee, as she had been warned, that skipping in the road may lead to her being run down.

'Sheep are especially sensitive to the exact moment of the turn of the tide. In this game, nine tethered sheep

react, pull on the stakes, jolt the chairs, and rattle the tea-cups. Bets are taken on the combined sensitivity of any line of three sheep read vertically, horizontally or diagonally. Since there are normally three tide turns every twenty-four hours, it is normal practice to take the best of three results. Reliable clocks, calendars and timetables are used to determine the accuracy of the sheep's forecast. In the game of sheep and tides, a referee should be appointed to determine fair play, distinguishing correct reactions from other interferences. On account of their special relationship to sheep, shepherds are disqualified.'

I ask Adam about the relationship between ritual and place. 'These kinds of movements within the landscape,' – we were talking about the games within 'Drowning by Numbers', in particular the vast complexity of Hangman's Cricket – 'are about a heightening of focus and perception, about the relationship between people and place becoming closer, but also they're about a getting 'out of it', losing oneself into the collective, and into the landscape. In the performing of self-conscious gestures within an environment we somehow inscribe ourselves onto our consciousness of the place. Which is why they should be constructed and reinvented within every community.'

He talks some more about an idea for a 'folk event' for our town – something involving all the alleyways – towards which I look back across the water. I think about what he is saying and the way that the words themselves seem to be performing the very thing that they are describing. Would it be possible to invent a new tradition in a town that already had its own festival, its own rituals?

'The important thing is that many of these folk events are dynamic and contemporary. They borrow and adapt and change all the time; they are not as pure as the folklorists would have us believe. For example the Burry Man,' – I check that here Adam is referring to the man covered in burrs who walks through a town centre, and who appears in *Plan for a Spell* – 'the Burry Man changes according to the whim of the few people involved every year, as does the burr costume, as does the precise date it takes place on. However, you can guarantee that, whenever it is or whatever he is wearing, they'll always visit the canteen of the local Hewlett Packard factory.'

We approach the hide through a strip in the reeds. The door is closed, and we can't see if anyone is in there. We walk towards the weather-silvered wood, up the steps, and open the door onto emptiness. Outside Adam notices that the front of the hide, which we have just approached, has been sprayed in lead shot. What games have been played here?

Some houses, farm buildings and a church. One of the houses is derelict, a tree growing out through one of its walls. I look through the empty window frame into an empty room. The wallpaper is the colour of mould, its paisley pattern almost following the shapes of the stains upon it, swarming around them, curling around each bloom, around each curved tear. A rabbit tears through the undergrowth; a kettle hangs from a branch. We enter the church and look at the collection of gifts available from the table: colouring books, pencils, chutneys. There is no electricity, simply unlit gas-lamps and candles.

We reach the pub much later than we thought and are nervous that they may no longer be serving, either drink but especially food (this was the point on the map to which we were walking, even if it wasn't the point of the walk). A pint of Guinness and pheasant casserole. The pub used to mark the point where a ferry crossed to the mainland, a straight line – not far – when the estuary mud slid below the water. But no more. Now new reasons must be made for coming this far, and as we walk out – rather happier than we walked in – we notice the numbered booths sheltered down into the bank, from which gunmen shoot at clay discs hurled into the air. Isn't this a kind of drawing also, a marking out in space? Red plastic cartridges emerge from the ground like spring bulbs.

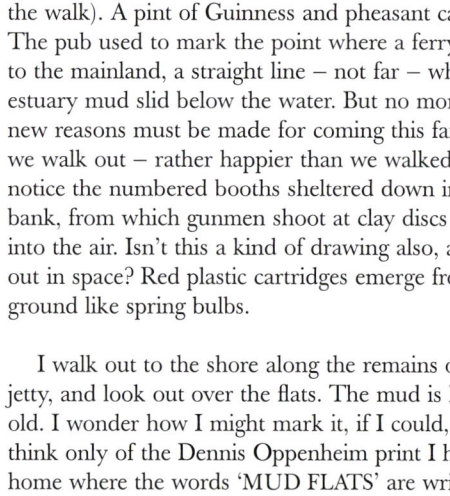

I walk out to the shore along the remains of the jetty, and look out over the flats. The mud is heavy, old. I wonder how I might mark it, if I could, and can think only of the Dennis Oppenheim print I have back home where the words 'MUD FLATS' are written is massive letters upon the surface of such a landscape, as though the information printed upon the map were transformed into actuality, making it literal rather than symbolic. I look over the water, along the line which the ferry used to travel, and try to imagine its wake, like the flattening of grass along a well-trodden path. Pylons mark the far shore like musical bars. I'm reminded of that old TV programme, 'The Changes', which scared, scarred, me as a child, in which the pylons were known as the 'bad wires' and a terrible sound forced all that heard it to smash all technological devices. The ribs of boats stick out of the brown mud. I allow myself a photograph.

but it might be placed exactly here

Plan for a Spell | 2001

We walk back to the car along a different route, along lanes and hedgerows, pheasants bursting from cover, their elastic-band whirr carrying them halfway across a field and hidden once more. There seems to be new ditches, and some new roadways, cutting across or swerving from the lines on our map. A row of mobile homes lie flattened on a piece of flat ground; a plastic barrel, now moved, leaves a yellow target on the grass at the edge of a field. Through a farmyard, and next to a holiday village, a stone marker stands a few feet high, slanted on its top a piece of square slate which has been engraved:

> *The First Powered Flight In*
> *This Country By A Briton*
> *J.T.C. Moore-Brabazon*
> *Took Place Near This Spot*
> *On*
> *2nd May 1909*

Perhaps it was the relative flatness of the land here, near the water's edge, which encouraged him to rise above it into one more dimension (another being time, history), to mark a trajectory across space, to draw a line with his shadow across the landscape.

We drive back to our town, from B to A, (and then M to A, actually), numbers 2231 to 249 to 2 to 299. And we pass a lorry which has been steadily losing its load of hay over the past few miles, and through which we have driven, like many others. I wonder whether I should signal to the driver but then maybe he knows what he is doing after all, performing a ritual, drawing a line, turning concrete to hay. Here, you're welcome to it.

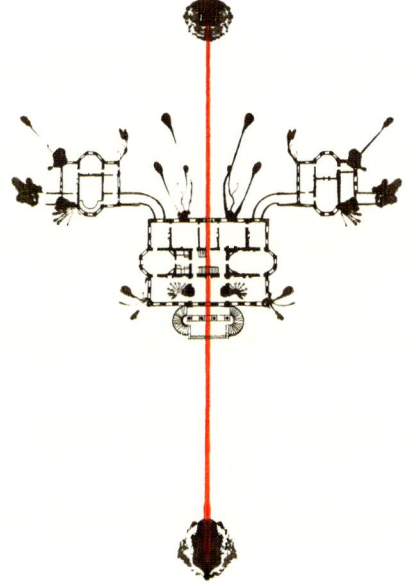

LIST OF WORKS INCLUDED IN THIS PUBLICATION

P4 **Plan for a Spell** | 2001
DVD and sound installation, infinite duration
[Detail – hill-top 'audio line']

P6 **From Beyond** | 1996
Video with sound, 5mins 15secs
[Detail – Jean Reve, an extra who appeared in Ken Russell's film 'The Devils,' (1971)]

P7 **Producing Siblings** | 1998
Video with sound, and thirteen framed images, 28 x 19.5cm
[Detail – page from *The Stage* newspaper and acrylic paint]

P8 **Involva** | 1995
Mixed media installation
Top   Involva (Act I)
     Pencil on contiboard, 21.8 x 31 x 1.5cm
Middle   Involva (Act I)
     Experience magazine, Vol.25, No.3, 33.5 x 40cm
Bottom   Involva (Act II)
     40.6 x 50.8cm each
[Detail – one from a series of seven C-type prints]
Private Collection, Italy

P9 **Red Herring** | 1996
The Most Hated Item of Clothing Convention
One from a series of six R-type prints, 40.6 x 30.5cm
Photography – Justin Westover

P9 **Reunion: *Salò*** | 1998
Video with sound, 8mins 10secs
12 framed C-type photographs, posters and plywood
29.8 x 21.1cm
[Detail – poster; off-set lithograph]

P10 **Plan for a Spell** | 2001
DVD and sound installation, infinite duration
[Detail – weaver]

Limbo Land | 2001
DVD and sound installation, 10mins 44secs
P11 [Production still]
P12 [Production still]
Commissioned by the Arts Council of England

P17 **Meeting** | 1999
Acid free paper, ink and paint, 59.3 x 41.7cm
[Detail – No.8 out of 15 versions]
Private collection, New York

P18 **Meeting** | 1999
Acid free paper, ink and paint
No.8 out of 15 versions, 59.3 x 41.7cm
Private collection, New York

P19 **The International God Look-Alike Contest** | 1995/96
Mixed media images
A series of 30 framed, 36.5 x 48.5cm
Top   [Detail – Andrey, Nikolaev, Ukraine. R-type print]
Left   [Detail – Jennifer, Manitoba, Canada. R-type print]
Middle   [Detail – Abdulluh, Calgary, Canada. R-type print]
Right   [Detail – Asomah, Sunyami, Ghana. R-type print]

P20 **Inverter (Clearance Sale)** | 1999
Adler advertisement, *Harpers & Queen*, November 1998
3 x advertisements from *Loot*, November 1998,
various dimensions. Edition of 35
Courtesy of Paul Stolper

Plan for a Spell | 2001
DVD and sound installation, infinite duration
P25 [Detail – wind turbines]
P26 [Detail – Burry Man, Queensferry, Scotland]
Courtesy Doc Rowe
P27 [Detail – foot and mouth pyres, Cumbria]
Courtesy Border TV
P28 [Detail – Demolition Derby, Roosecote Raceway, Barrow in Furness]
P29 [Detail – Uppies and Downies, Workington]
Courtesy Border TV
P30 [Detail – stumps of 'The Wicker Man' (1973), Isle of Whithorn, Scotland]
P31 [Detail – hill-top 'audio line']

Reunion: *Salò* | 1998
Video with sound, 8mins 10secs
12 framed C-type photographs, posters and plywood
P33 One from a series of 12 C-type prints of 'doubles', 50.8 x 40.7cm

P34 **A Place for *The End*** | 1999
DVD with sound installation, 10mins
Eight framed b&w photographs, 50 x 80cm
Top   [Detail – Hockley flyover]
Middle Left [Detail – field off Corwen Croft]
Middle Right [Detail – canal railway bridge]
Bottom Left [Details – installation of plaque outside 104, Nechells Place]
Bottom Right [Detail – outside 104, Nechells Place]
Commissioned by Ikon Gallery, Birmingham

P36 **Plan for a Spell** | 2001
DVD and sound installation, infinite duration
[Detail – Ottery St Mary, tar barrels]
Courtesy of Doc Rowe

P37 **Plan for a Spell** | 2001
Notes for the positioning of subtitles

P39 **Loose Disclaimer** | 2000
Six 1 minute video sequences added to the ends
of video films rented from video stores,
six photographs and certificate
Left [Detail – Still No.1, 50 x 76cm, R-type photograph]
Right [Detail – Certificate, Pigment on paper, 29 x 21cm]

Better Scenery | 2000
Mixed media installation
P40 [Detail – Arizona desert]
Commissioned by Camden Arts Centre, London
P41 [Detail – Sainsbury's car park, Finchley Road, London]
Commissioned by Camden Arts Centre, London

Better Scenery | 2001
Mixed media installation
P42 [Detail – Grizedale Forest, Cumbria, UK]
Courtesy of Grizedale Arts and Galleria Franco Noero, Torino
P43 [Detail – Italdesign factory, Torino, Italy]
Courtesy of Grizedale Arts and Galleria Franco Noero, Torino

P47 **Plan for a Spell** | 2001
DVD and sound installation, infinite duration
[Detail – computer game]

P48 **Flasher** | 1998
Video, R-type photograph and certificate
[Detail – 1 minute video sequence added to the end
of a video film rented from a video store]

P50 **Plan for a Spell** | 2001
DVD and sound installation
Infinite duration
[Detail – Burry Man, Queensferry, Scotland]
courtesy Doc Rowe

P51 **As the Crow Flies** | 2000
Video and drawing
[Detail – ink on paper, 59.3 x 41.7cm]

P56 **Plan for a Spell** | 2001
DVD and sound installation
Infinite duration
[Detail – street coincidence]

ADDITIONAL ACKNOWLEDGEMENTS

Limbo Land | 2001
Nick Fenton – editor, Tim Barker – sound design,
Lucy Tillett, Janet Hewlett-Davies and Dermot Kearney,
Sebastien Sharples, Gary Thomas and VET

Plan for a Spell | 2001
Doc Rowe, Renee de Luycker at the Digital Group,
Tim Barker – sound design, Julian McDonald at Townhouse
Studios, Matthew Southern, Steve Wilson and Dave Griffiths
at ICDC, Liverpool, Stuart Baker, Paul Ayer

With thanks to the following collections for works reproduced:
Tate Modern, The British Council, The Saatchi Collection,
Arts Council Collection, FRAC Languedoc Roussillon,
Stephen Bury, Auckland Art Gallery
and all private collections

Photography
P9 (Red Herring) and P48 (Flasher) by Justin Westover
P11 by Phil Pleasants
P45-50 additional photographs by Jeremy Millar

ADAM CHODZKO

1965	Born in London
1985-88	University of Manchester, BA (Hons) History of Art
1992-94	Goldsmiths' College, London, MA Fine Art
	Lives and works in Whitstable and London

SELECTED ONE-PERSON EXHIBITIONS

2002	Fabrica, Brighton
2001	Galleria Franco Noero, Turin
	Sandroni Rey Gallery, Venice, California
	Els Hanappe Underground, Athens
2000	Accademia Britannica, Rome
1999	Galleria Franco Noero, Turin
	Ikon Gallery, Birmingham
1998	Gallery II, Bradford
	Northern Gallery of Contemporary Art, Sunderland
	Viewpoint Gallery, Salford
1996	Lotta Hammer, London
	Milch, London

SELECTED GROUP EXHIBITIONS

2002	*Life is Beautiful*, Laing Art Gallery, Newcastle-upon-Tyne*
	Tabu, Kunsthaus Baselland, Switzerland*
2001	*The Seat with The Clearest View*,
	Grey Matter Contemporary Art, Sydney
	Bright Paradise, 1st Auckland Triennial,
	Auckland Art Gallery, New Zealand*
	Night on Earth, Städtische Ausstellungshalle
	am Hawerkamp, Münster.*
	Liquor, Trafo Galeria, Budapest*
	Helle Nacht, Bottmingen, Baselland
	Sacred and Profane, Mappin Art Gallery, Sheffield,
	touring to York City Art Gallery*
2000	*Dreammachines* (curated by Susan Hiller), Dundee
	Contemporary Arts, touring to Mappin Art Gallery,
	Sheffield; Camden Arts Centre, London; Glyn Vivian
	Art Gallery, Swansea*
	Found Wanting, The Contemporary, Atlanta, USA
	Somewhere Near Vada, Project Art Centre, Dublin*
	Artifice, Deste Foundation, Athens*
	Face On, Site Gallery, Sheffield; touring to Milton Keynes
	Gallery; Open Eye Gallery, Liverpool and Stills, Edinburgh*
	Places in Mind (with Stan Douglas and Elizabeth Macgill),
	Ormeau Baths Gallery, Belfast
1999	*Sleuth*, ffotogallery, Cardiff; touring to Oriel Mostyn,
	Llandudno and Barbican Centre, London
1998	*A to Z*, Approach Gallery, London
	Wrapped, Vestsjællands Kunstmuseum, Sorø, Denmark*
1997	*It Always Jumps Back and Finds its Own Way*,
	Stichting de Appel, Amsterdam*
	3 wege zum See, Künstlerhaus Klagenfurt, Austria*
	Sensation, Royal Academy, London*; touring to Museum für
	Gegenwart, Berlin, and Brooklyn Museum of Art, New York
	at one remove, Henry Moore Institute, Leeds*
1996	*21 Days of Darkness*, Transmission Gallery, Glasgow
	Perfect, Jan Mot and Oscar van den Boogaard, Brussells
1995	*Every Time I See You*, Galleri Nicolai Wallner, Malmö
	Zombie Golf, Bank, London
	General Release, British Council selection for Venice Biennale,
	Scoula San Pasquale, Venice*
	Brilliant, Walker Arts Center, Minneapolis*
1994	*High Fidelity* (with Simon Patterson), Kohji Ogura Gallery,
	Nagoya, touring to Röntgen Kunst Institut, Tokyo*
	WM Karaoke, Portikus, Frankfurt
1993	*Making People Disappear*, Cubitt Street Gallery, London
	Okay Behaviour, 303 Gallery, New York
	Wonderful Life, Lisson Gallery, London
1992-93	*Instructions Received*, Gio Marconi, Milan*
1991	*City Racing*, London

* exhibition publication

SELECTED PROJECTS

2001	*Slipstream*, web work for Film and Video Umbrella:
	www.slipstream.uk.net
	Nothing (edited by Graham Gussin),
	August Publications, pp98-99
1999	*Moonstruck*, 'tate', No.18, Summer, pp34-36
	A Place for 'The End', off-site project for
	Ikon Gallery, Birmingham
	Better Scenery, (Camden, London and Arizona Desert, USA)
	off-site project for Camden Arts Centre, London
1997	*Le Petit Prince Recall*, with Pierre Huyghe, 'Mobile TV', Dijon
1996	Cover page, 'frieze', November 1996
	Red Herring, artist's project,
	'Dazed & Confused', No.27, pp60-65
1994	*Slow Down Skin Shed*, in 'British Art Special',
	'The Face', No.68, May, pp56-72

BIBLIOGRAPHY

SELECTED BOOKS AND CATALOGUES

2002 *Romanov*, published by Book Works, London
2001 *Bright Paradise*, 1st Auckland Triennial, Auckland Art
 Gallery, New Zealand, texts by Allan Smith, et al
 Art for All (edited by Mark Wallinger and Mary Warnock),
 Peer, pp64&94
 Out of the Bubble, edited by John Carson
 and Susannah Silver, pp32-36
 Night on Earth, Städtische Ausstellungshalle
 am Hawerkamp, Münster
2000 *Somewhere Near Vada*, Project Art Centre, Dublin,
 texts by Jaki Irvine and Shirley MacWilliam
 Dreammachines, National Touring Exhibitions,
 text by Susan Hiller
 Face On, Black Dog Publishing,
 texts by Craig Richardson et al
1999 *Adam Chodzko*, August Publications,
 texts by Jennifer Higgie and Michael Bracewell
1998 *Wrapped*, Vestsjælands Kunstmuseum, Sorø, Denmark
1997 *It Always Jumps Back and Finds its Own Way*,
 Stichting de Appel, Amsterdam
 texts by K Schippers and Cosima Rainer
 3 wege zum See, Künstlerhaus Klagenfurt, Austria
 Matthew Collings, *Blimey*,
 pp124, 126, 132-133
 Sensation, Royal Academy
 at one remove, Henry Moore Institute, Leeds,
 text by Penelope Curtis
1996 *British Waves*, British Festival, Rome,
 text by Mario Condognato
1995 *General Release*, British Council, Venice Biennale,
 texts by Gregor Muir and James Roberts
1993 *High Fidelity*, Kohji Ogura Gallery, Nagoya, Japan,
 text by James Roberts

SELECTED ARTICLES AND REVIEWS

2001 Michael Wilson, *These Days*,
 Untitled, No.25, Summer 2001, pp7-9
2000 Jonathon Jones, *Arizona, NW3*,
 The Guardian, 15 January, p25
 Michael Wilson, *Sleuth*,
 Art Monthly, No.234, March, p34
 Massimo Carboni, *Adam Chodzko*,
 Art Forum, No.8, April, p149
 Jonathon Jones, *Adam Chodzko*,
 frieze, No.52, May, p95
 Michael Corris, *Face On*,
 Art Monthly, No.240, October, pp30-31

1999 Adam Chodzko in discussion with Robin Rimbaud,
 everything, No.24, pp16-20
 Laura Cherbini, *I video crudeli di...*,
 Il Giornale, Italy, 24 May
 Charles Darwent, *Who do they think they are?*,
 Independent on Sunday, 4 July
 Interview with David Barrett,
 Art Club, Habitat, pp16-22
 Looking in the Wrong Place, interview with John Slyce,
 Dazed & Confused, No.57, August, pp100-106
 David Barrett, *Adam Chodzko*,
 Art Monthly, No.229, September, pp29-31
 John Slyce, *Adam Chodzko*,
 Flash Art International, 32, No.208, October, pp120-121
1998 Jonathan Jones, *Faces of Evil*,
 The Guardian, 18 August
1997 Tom Lubbock, *Who Are They Pointing At?*,
 The Independent, 18 September
 Teresa Macri, *In cerco di 'Salò'*,
 il manifesto, 8 November
1996 Susan Corrigan, *Twisted Mister*,
 i-D, No.48, January, p10
 Kevin Jackson, *BritPop Art*,
 Arena, April, pp60-66
 Kate Spicer, *Nearly God*,
 The Face, No.93, June
 Patricia Bickers, *The Young Devils*,
 Art Press, No.214, p34
 David Burrows, *Adam Chodzko*,
 Art Monthly, No.198, July/August, pp28-29
 James Roberts, *Adult Fun*,
 frieze, No.31, pp62-67
 Diane Eddisford, *>alt.zombie.golf.the.earth*,
 Mute, No.2, Summer, p2
 Simon Grant, *Playing God*,
 Art Monthly, No.189, September, pp28-29
 Roberta Smith, *A Show of Moderns Seeking to Shock*,
 New York Times, 25 November
1994 Julia Cassim, *Chodzko, Patterson Weak on Public Participation*,
 The Japan Times, 13 February
 Kaori Makabe, *London Strikes Back*,
 Bijutsu Techo, Tokyo, Vol.46, No.688, pp53-55
 Ekow Eshun, *British Art Special*,
 The Face, No.68, May, pp56-72
1993 Andrew Renton, *Adam Chodzko*,
 Flash Art, Milan, March-April
 Simon Grant, *Making People Disappear*,
 What's On, London, 21 April
 Richard Shone, *God's Bods and Odd Bods*,
 The Observer, London, 8 August
 Rob Legge, *The Faces of God*,
 The Independent on Sunday, London, 19 September, pp40-41

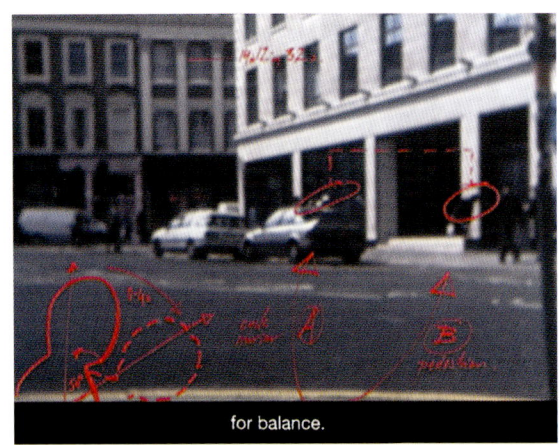

Adam Chodzko: Plans and Spells
Published by Film and Video Umbrella
Edited by Steven Bode
Designed by Richard Bonner-Morgan
Printed by Trichrom Ltd

Published to accompany the Film and Video Umbrella touring exhibition, *Plan for a Spell* by Adam Chodzko, commissioned by Film and Video Umbrella and Mappin Art Gallery, Sheffield for the exhibition *Sacred and Profane*

Publication supported by the National Touring Programme of the Arts Council of England. With additional support from Central St Martins College of Art and Design

Adam Chodzko would like to thank – Steven Bode, Mike Jones, Caroline Smith, Bevis Bowden and everyone else at Film and Video Umbrella, Richard Bonner-Morgan, Adam Sutherland and Grizedale Arts, Franco Noero, Els Hanappe, Lottie Child, James Roberts, Juliet and Justin Chodzko, Clio Barnard and Seth

Thanks also to – Julie Milne and Sarah Brown at Mappin Art Gallery, Matthew Miller at Fabrica, Renee de Luycker and Peter Wooliscroft at the Digital Group

Printed in an edition of 1,000

ISBN 0-9538634-7-6
©2002, Film and Video Umbrella, the artist and the authors

Film and Video Umbrella
52 Bermondsey Street London SE1 3UD
T 020 7407 7755 F 020 7407 7766
E info@fvu.co.uk W www.fvumbrella.com